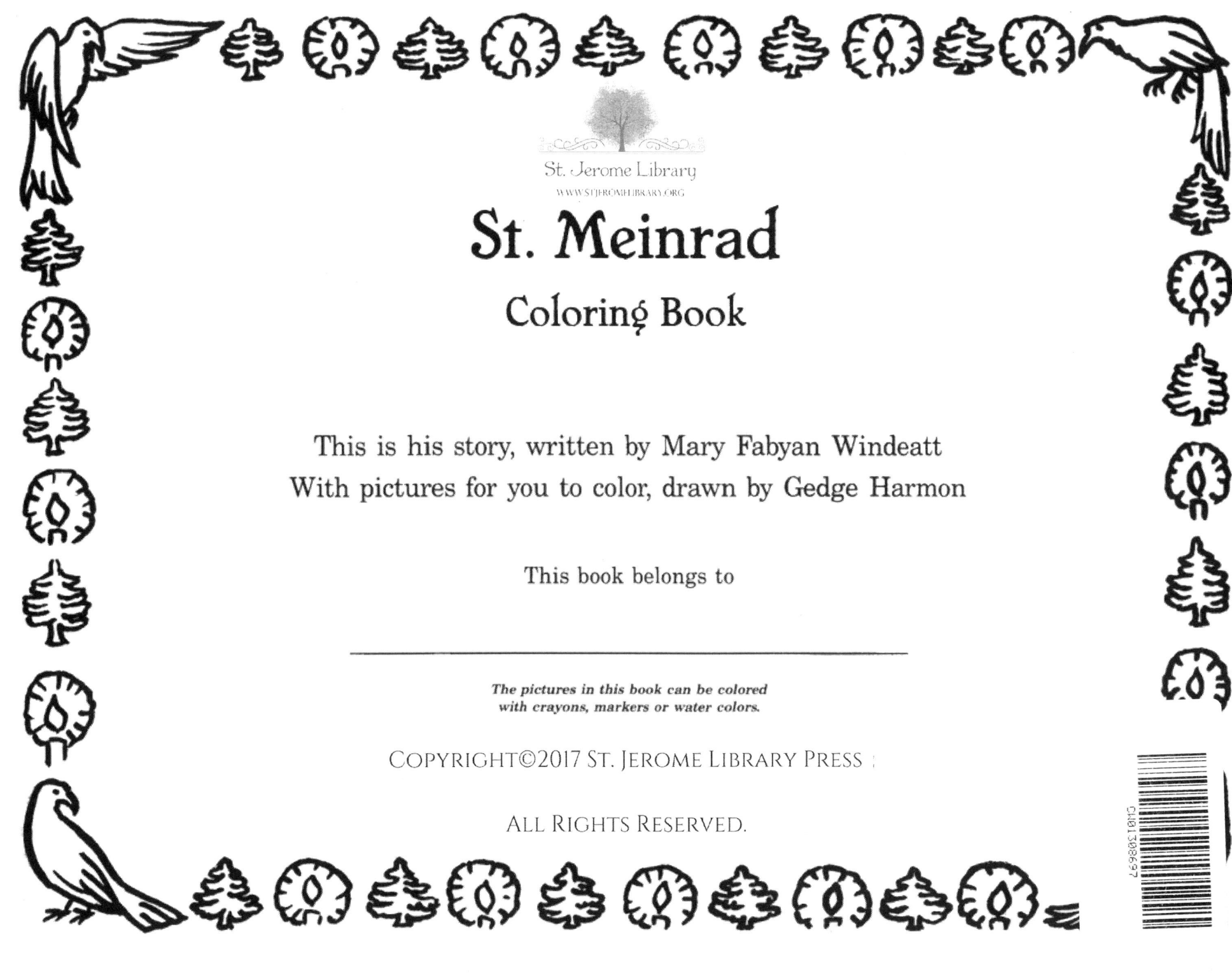

St. Jerome Library
WWW.STJEROMELIBRARY.ORG

St. Meinrad

Coloring Book

This is his story, written by Mary Fabyan Windeatt
With pictures for you to color, drawn by Gedge Harmon

This book belongs to

_____

*The pictures in this book can be colored
with crayons, markers or water colors.*

Copyright©2017 St. Jerome Library Press

All Rights Reserved.

CHAPTER ONE

ONE day in the year 809 there was great excitement in a certain castle in what is now southwestern Germany. Twelve-year-old Meginrat (whose name was more easily pronounced Meinrad), was about to leave home for the first time. He was to enter the famous school of the Benedictine monks on the island of Reichenau, in Lake Constance.

"It's the best school in the Empire," declared his father boastfully. "The boy will learn many useful things there."

His mother hesitated, dabbing at her tearful eyes. "I know," she said. "But Meinrad's still so young! And it's such a long trip to Reichenau, with wild animals in the woods along the way, even thieves and murderers...."

The father laughed. "Did you forget I'm taking the boy to Reichenau myself? Let man or beast even try to harm him, and my sword shall soon settle the score."

Young Meinrad also reassured his mother, reminding her that God had absolute power over every living creature. Besides, hadn't their cousin Erlebald (one of the holiest monks at Reichenau), promised to pray that they should have a safe journey?

"Everything's going to be all right, Mother," he insisted cheerfully. "Really and truly!"

CHAPTER TWO

IN the days that followed, the boy's courage never wavered. What joy to have been accepted as a student in the school of the Benedictine monks, the greatest scholars in Europe! Already he knew a little of their founder, the kindly Saint Benedict who had gone home to God some two hundred and sixty-two years before, and whose monasteries were now so famous. But at Reichenau he would undoubtedly learn much more. And make new and interesting friends, too.

Such thoughts filled the lad's mind as he and his father made their way through the deep forests, so that he was scarcely aware of the hardships of the journey. Then one day his heart gave a great leap. He had caught sight of Lake Constance, ringed about with pine and spruce, and sparkling like a sapphire in the sun.

"Father! Do you see what I see?" he burst out eagerly.

The man smiled. "Yes, son. Possibly even more."

Meinrad gazed in astonishment. What could his father see that he could not? Then he saw it. A small boat, moored at the water's edge, was taking on passengers and baggage.

"That boat goes directly to Reichenau, Meinrad," explained the father hastily. "We'd better hurry if we don't want to be left behind."

CHAPTER THREE

MEINRAD never forgot his first ride across Lake Constance to the Benedictine monastery on the island of Reichenau. Or the warm welcome extended by his cousin, Father Erlebald. And when just a few weeks had passed, he felt completely at home in his new surroundings.

"It's just as though I'd never lived anywhere else," he reflected.

The other boys were also happy. And busy, too, for Reichenau was full of activity. Long ago Saint Benedict had written in his Holy Rule that the monastic day was to be divided between prayer and work. And what a variety of work there was to be done! Fields had to be tilled, vineyards planted, the cattle cared for, timber cut, meals cooked, and there were also a great number of other tasks to be accomplished each day. And though the monks did most of the heavy work, their students helped when lessons were over.

Naturally Father Erlebald was delighted that Meinrad was so happy at Reichenau. Could it be possible that this young cousin had a vocation to the religious life, too? That when his schooling was over he might even decide to become a priest? How wonderful that would be!

"I must pray for that intention," he told himself thoughtfully. "And let his parents know about my hopes."

CHAPTER FOUR

SINCE Meinrad's parents were both devout Christians, they joined their prayers to those of Father Erlebald that God should see fit to grant their son the priceless gift of a vocation to the priesthood. And in the year 822, when Meinrad was twenty-five, these prayers were finally answered. Then, in the beautiful church of the island monastery, Meinrad was ordained a priest. That same year, upon the death of the Abbot of Reichenau, the community elected Father Erlebald to take his place.

Meinrad had always had a deep affection for Father Erlebald, and now he rejoiced at the great honor which had come to his kinsman. Henceforth, as Abbot of Reichenau, he was to be God's representative for monks and students alike. All authority would be vested in him. He was the father of the monastic family, and was to be obeyed as God Himself. In return, he would care for his subjects in justice and love. He would never have any favorites. Above all, he would help everyone he met to want to be kind and good, too.

"What a responsibility!" Meinrad often thought. "I must pray for our new Father Abbot as I've never prayed before...."

CHAPTER SIX

MEINRAD remained at Benken for four years. Then it was decided to discontinue the boys' school there. A wonderful thought now came to his mind. Perhaps Abbot Erlebald would permit him to be a hermit? Long ago such men as Antony, Paul and Hilarion had felt that they could best serve their fellowman by lives of prayerful solitude. God had blessed their decision, and now they were glorious saints in heaven.

But Abbot Erlebald was not quite sure that Meinrad was meant to be a hermit. "That kind of life is most unusual and difficult," he declared, when Meinrad told him of his hopes. "And not exactly suited to a monk, my son. In fact, your whole plan may have a tinge of selfishness to it."

Meinrad hesitated. "You think I want to escape from further responsibility, Father Abbot? That I'm running away from life with the brethren?"

"Well—"

"Oh, no! That's not it at all. I want to pray for my brethren—really pray! And if I have no active duties, if I can give all my time to loving and praising God, He will surely bless the prayers I offer for others."

CHAPTER SEVEN

MEINRAD'S sincerity was so evident that finally the Abbot gave him permission to lead a solitary life on nearby Mount Etzel. Here the young priest was supremely happy, despite many hardships. However, after a time certain peasants began to spread the word that he was a saint and wonderworker, and the curious came in increasing numbers to seek him out. This was a cause of much concern to Meinrad. Thus, when seven years had passed—

"I'm not really a hermit here at all," he decided. "With Father Abbot's permission, I'll move deeper into the forest where it'll be harder for people to find me. Then I'll have time to pray as I should."

So in 835, when he was thirty-eight years old, Meinrad built a second hermitage and made a new effort to lead a life of prayer and sacrifice for others. But once again he was not quite alone in the wilderness. Two young ravens, grateful for the food and care given them, became his constant companions.

"Ah, dear Lord, thank You for these little friends," he often prayed. "And for this happy solitude! But don't let me grow selfish in it. Bless all the brethren at Reichenau and Benken. Bless my friends and family in the world, too. And help me always to know and love Your Holy Will...."

CHAPTER EIGHT

PRESENTLY Meinrad realized that he was not to pass his days in complete solitude after all. Once again his hermitage had been discovered. Once again men and women were seeking him out and asking his prayers for this and that intention.

"Dear Father, my wife is dreadfully ill! Won't you please ask God to cure her?"

"I'm blind, Father. In heaven's name, tell me how I'm to make a living...."

"I have six little ones at home, Father, and the crops failed last year. Couldn't you spare me some food?"

"And me, Father?"

"And me?"

Touched beyond words by the plight of so many sick and discouraged, Meinrad bade each of his visitors be of good heart. Yes, he would remember their intentions in his Mass and prayers. He would ask Our Lady for help, too, in the little chapel he had built adjoining his hermitage. As for food and clothing—

"My friends, God's Mother can do all things for us if we just have faith in her," he declared. "Come, now—let's kneel down and tell her what we need."

CHAPTER NINE

SOON Meinrad's woodland hermitage had become a favorite place of pilgrimage for young and old. Wonderful favors were granted there, people reported. In fact, Our Lady's statue (which had been given to Meinrad by a holy Abbess named Heilwiga), seemed to have miraculous powers. As a result, many pilgrims felt it only right to leave offerings at the hermitage in thanksgiving for favors received.

"Father Meinrad's a poor man," they said. "He can use this money to buy a few comforts for himself."

"A decent bed, for instance?"

"That's right. He's been sleeping on the floor ever since he came here."

"Perhaps he could use some warm winter clothes, too."

"Of course he could. It gets very cold in these woods."

But Meinrad had no wish for comforts, and rapidly disposed of all offerings—money, jewels, food, clothing—among the poor. The result? All hell was enraged by such Christlike charity.

"Something's got to be done about this wretched hermit!" fumed the Devil. "Why, he's getting holier all the time! And helping others to be holier, too. Oh, if I could just think of some way to get rid of him...."

CHAPTER TEN

BUT the years passed, and all the Devil's plots were of no avail. He could not frighten Meinrad, even though he frequently appeared to him under the most hideous forms. Nor could he discourage him in his efforts to make Our Lady known and loved. Then one day, when Meinrad was sixty-four years old, the Devil hit upon a plan. He would inflame the hearts of certain men with jealousy! He would put it into their heads to rob the holy hermit of the gifts left with him, even to kill!

On the morning of January 21, 861, as Meinrad was offering Mass in his little chapel, God let him know of the Devil's plan. Even now two ruffians were approaching through the snow, bent on robbery and murder.

Meinrad turned pale. "Father, forgive them!" he whispered. Then, bending low over the Sacred Host: "They know not what they do...."

However, a moment later he was wholly at peace. What matter that death might be at hand? In a little while he would be seeing the saints, Our Lady, God! Calmly he continued the Holy Sacrifice, made his thanksgiving, then went to answer a savage pounding at his door.

"Yes, friends?" he said, smiling at two evil-faced strangers standing on the threshold. "Is there anything I can do for you?"

CHAPTER ELEVEN

THE men, armed with clubs, hesitated only a moment. "We've lost our way in the woods," announced the first, smirking at his companion. "We thought that perhaps—"

Meinrad nodded encouragingly. "Of course I'll be glad to help," he said. "But first, won't you come inside and visit Our Lady's chapel? Then have some food and drink?"

The ruffians winked at each other, stamped in and out of the chapel, then slumped down at a nearby table. What a fool this hermit was! Did he open his door to everyone who knocked? Did he treat even men armed with clubs as brothers?

Meinrad calmly and courteously ministered to his guests' needs. When they had eaten and drunk their fill, he presented them with some warm clothing. But at this the men leapt angrily to their feet.

"Enough of that, old man!" snapped the first. "Where's the gold and silver you've hidden away? That's what we came for."

Slowly Meinrad folded his hands. "Gold and silver, friend? Ah, I have nothing like that here."

"Liar!" roared the second, brandishing his club. "Everyone knows the pilgrims have made you generous gifts for years. Speak up now, or it'll go hard with you!"

CHAPTER TWELVE

MEINRAD shook his head. "My gifts have always been given to the poor," he said quietly. "There is nothing valuable here." Then, with a little smile: "But why waste time in talking? Whatever you have come to do, do it quickly. When you have finished, take the two candles from the table. Place one at my head, the other at my feet. Light them, and may God have mercy on your souls...."

At once the two men set upon Meinrad in savage fury. "Wretch! You'd try to mock us, would you?"

"Take that!"

"And that!"

A low groan escaped Meinrad's lips as the savage blows began to fall upon him. Blood gushed from his mouth, and he toppled to the floor. But, until they were quite sure he was dead, the thieves continued to use their clubs unmercifully. However, when they had made a search of the hermitage and found nothing of value, a strange panic seized them.

"Maybe the old man was a saint after all!" stammered the first. "Quick! Put lighted candles about him as he asked...."

So they set out the candles. But as they started to the chapel to find a taper, a terrifying event took place. The candle they had just placed at Meinrad's head leapt into light!

CHAPTER THIRTEEN

FOR a moment the murderers stood in terror. Then they stumbled blindly toward the door. "Make for the village!" gasped the first. "It's an angel who lighted that candle...."

"Yes! Yes! He'll burn us to death if he can...."

But the two criminals had struggled only a short distance through the snow when the air was rent by the harsh screaming of Meinrad's pet ravens. Diving and wheeling in ever-narrowing circles, they finally swooped down to attack the terrified fugitives with beak and claw. And try as they would to defend themselves, the men were soon torn and bleeding.

"Help! Help!" they cried. "These birds have gone mad!"

Their cries were soon heard by a passing woodcutter, who came to look. But unable to believe that Meinrad's well-known pets had turned savage without cause, he remained for a few moments in hiding behind some trees, and watched. Then he quickly went off and found his brother and told him what he had seen.

"Hear Father Meinrad's ravens screaming?" he demanded breathlessly. "Something's wrong at the hermitage! Quick, find the men and follow them while I go to see what I can do—"

CHAPTER FOURTEEN

BEFORE nightfall everyone knew that the holy hermit Meinrad had been cruelly murdered. But the ruffians who had killed him would soon pay for their crime. Pursued all the way to Zurich by the infuriated ravens, they had been easily caught, and even now were awaiting execution.

"Those two deserve to be burned at the stake," was the general opinion. "Imagine, killing a poor old man who had been so kind to them...."

The monks of Reichenau sorrowfully carried Meinrad's body to their monastery for burial. After that, his hermitage remained without a tenant for forty-five years. Then, in 906, a holy Bishop named Benno made it his home. Bishop Benno's occupancy was followed, in 934, by that of another holy Bishop named Eberhard. Bishop Eberhard eventually founded a community of Benedictine monks where Meinrad had lived, then built a complete church around his hermitage and chapel.

"Everything will be dedicated to Our Lady of Einsiedeln," it was finally decided.

Einsiedeln? Certain visitors were a bit puzzled. Just what did that mean? But soon everything was clear. Einsiedeln came from the German word meaning "hermit." And what more fitting name for the new monastery than "Our Lady of the Hermit"? Especially since the very statue of the Queen of Heaven which Meinrad had loved and honored was now enthroned there?

CHAPTER FIFTEEN

ON October 6, 1039, Meinrad's main relics were finally brought from Reichenau to the Abbey of Our Lady of Einsiedeln, and his name was added to the list of saints by Pope Benedict the Ninth. Many favors were reported by those who prayed before these relics. So many, in fact, that the little chapel in the Abbey church (where the relics and Meinrad's statue of Our Lady were kept), came to be referred to as "The Chapel of Graces."

As time passed, the Abbey of Our Lady of Einsiedeln became even more famous, not only in Switzerland but in faraway America, too. For centuries it had been the resting place of a saint and martyr, but now it was something more—one of the greatest centers of piety, learning and culture to be found anywhere.

Thus, in the spring of 1852, in Jasper, Indiana, forty-two-year-old Father Joseph Kundek determined to visit Einsiedeln and beg for a great favor through the intercession of Saint Meinrad: namely, that the Abbot of Einsiedeln would send some monks as missionaries to America.

"Saint Meinrad, do let things turn out that way!" he prayed. "Who knows how many souls might be saved if your brethren were to settle in Indiana? After all, the poor people here do need priests so much!"

CHAPTER SIXTEEN

FATHER KUNDEK'S pilgrimage to distant Switzerland was blessed by God. When he arrived at Einsiedeln on June 15 of that same year, 1852, the Abbot promised that two of his monks, Father Ulrich Christen and Father Bede O'Connor, would go to Indiana to see what could be done for the people there. If conditions were favorable, they would start work on a new monastery dedicated to Saint Meinrad.

The two monks from Einsiedeln set out on December 20, arriving in Vincennes, Indiana, on February 17, 1853. The Bishop gave them a warm welcome, and soon plans were under way for Saint Meinrad's Priory. A site was chosen some fifty miles east of Evansville, amid the forests of Spencer County, and on March 21, the Feast of Saint Benedict, 1854, a simple log cabin there was solemnly dedicated to the service of God.

"Well, Saint Meinrad has now come to America," said Father Ulrich. "Let's hope he helps us with our work."

"He will," said Father Bede confidently.

But neither priest ever dreamed of the glorious future Saint Meinrad actually had in store for their foundation. That one day, in the place of the little log cabin, would stand Saint Meinrad Archabbey, one of the most important religious houses in the United States: the home of more than 200 Benedictine priests, Brothers and Oblates, and the school where some 1,800 other priests, including 69 Monsignori, 11 Bishops and one Archbishop had received their seminary training.

Windeatt Coloring Book Series Titles

Vol. 1 St. Teresa of Avila
Vol. 2 St. Pius X
Vol. 3 St. Philomena
Vol. 4 St. Meinrad
Vol. 5 St. Maria Goretti
Vol. 6 Kateri of the Mohawks
Vol 7 St. Joan of Arc
Vol. 8 St. Francis of Assisi
Vol. 9 St. Frances Cabrini
Vol. 10 St. Dominic Savio
Vol. 11 St. Christopher
Vol. 12 St. Anthony of Padua

Vol. 13 Our Lady of Banneux
Vol. 14 Our Lady of Beuraing
Vol. 15 Our Lady of Fatima
Vol. 16 Our Lady of Guadalupe
Vol. 17 Our Lady of Knock
Vol. 18 Our Lady of La Salette
Vol. 19 Our Lady of Lourdes
Vol. 20 Our Lady of the Miraculous Medal
Vol. 21 Our Lady of Pellevoisin
Vol. 22 Our Lady of Pontmain

Vol. 23 The Brown Scapular
Vol. 24 The Rosary

Printed in Great Britain
by Amazon